Ask Dr. K. Fisher

about Reptiles

Written by
Claire Llewellyn

Illustrated by
Kate Sheppard

KINGFISHER
NEW YORK

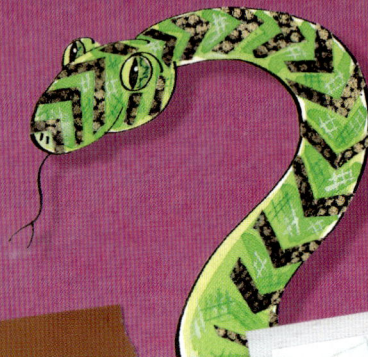

Claire

Kate

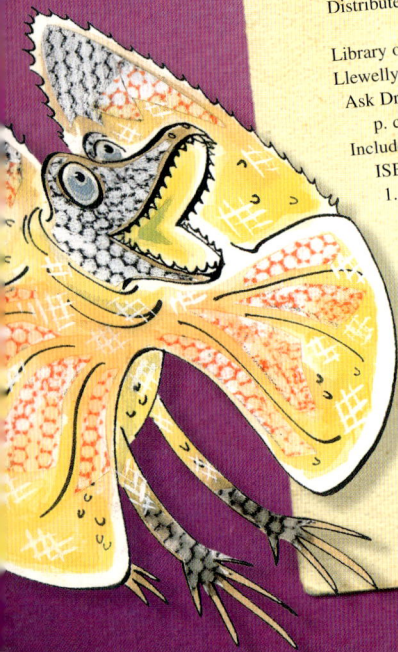

Consultant: David Burnie

Copyright © 2008 by Macmillan Publishers Ltd.
Text and concept © 2008 by Claire Llewellyn
KINGFISHER
Published in the United States by Kingfisher, an imprint of Henry Holt
and Company LLC, 175 Fifth Avenue, New York, New York 10010.
First published in Great Britain by Kingfisher Publications plc, an imprint
of Macmillan Children's Books, London.

Distributed in Canada by H. B. Fenn and Company Ltd.

Library of Congress Cataloging-in-Publication Data
Llewellyn, Claire.
    Ask Dr. K. Fisher about reptiles / Claire Llewellyn.—1st American ed.
        p. cm.
    Includes index.
    ISBN 978-0-7534-6272-0
    1. Reptiles—Juvenile literature. I. Title.
    QL644.2.L638 2008
    597.9—dc22   2007047430

ISBN: 978-0-7534-6272-0

Kingfisher books are available for special promotions and premiums.
For details contact: Director of Special Markets, Holtzbrinck Publishers.

First American Edition October 2008
Printed in China
10 9 8 7 6 5 4 3 2 1
1TR/0608/TECH/SCHOY/157MA/C

To my friend Tali—C. L.
For Potae—K. S.

Kingfisher

Henry Holt and Company

175 Fifth Avenue

New York, NY 10010

Ask Dr. K. Fisher about . . .

Hot, hot, hot!

frog

THE EVERGLADES
AUG. 23RD
MAIL

Dear Dr. K. Fisher,
I'm an alligator, and I'm a real sun worshiper. I spend hours sunbathing every day. But I know the sun is very strong. Do you think I'm overdoing it?

Sun Lover,
in the swamp

Dr. K. Fisher

1 Diving-in-the-Water

Birdsville 54321

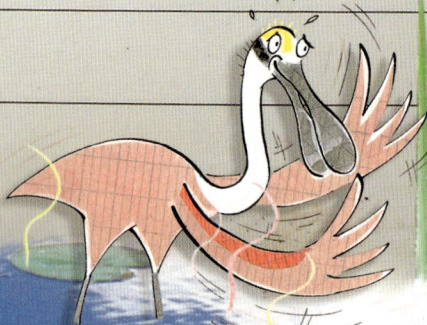

alligator
warming up

spoonbills

Dr. K. Fisher
Any problem solved!
1 Diving-in-the-Water
Birdsville 54321

Dear **Sun Lover,**

All reptiles need plenty of sunlight—that's because you are cold-blooded and your body temperature changes along with your surroundings. In the morning after a long, cool night, your body feels lazy and slow— it can't even digest your food. So it's very important that you bask in the sun. As your body warms up, you will have more energy. If you still feel too warm, open your mouth and let the breeze blow inside.

Alternatively, move into the shade or take a dip in the cool swamp water.

Best wishes,

Dr. K. Fisher

cooling off!

5

Here's a gecko that's had a shock

A lucky escape!

Dear Dr. K. Fisher,

I'm a gecko, and I've had a terrible accident. The other day I was attacked by a snake, which bit off my tail. I managed to escape, but I really loved that tail. Now I don't want to face my friends without it. How will I ever get back my confidence?

Lost My Tail,
in the tropics

tree snake

gecko

6

Dr. K. Fisher
Any problem solved!
1 Diving-in-the-Water
Birdsville 54321

Dear **Lost My Tail,**

When predators attack a lizard like you, they often grab onto your long, skinny tail. But they don't know about your great defense—your tail then breaks off and wiggles on the ground! It's a terrific trick that surprises predators and gives lizards the chance to escape. I have good news for you: your tail will regrow over the next few weeks. It might be a slightly different color and it will contain rubbery cartilage instead of hard bone.

Still, a tail's a tail!

Yours sincerely,

Dr. K. Fisher

new tail!

Turn the page for **more** about reptile defenses . . .

7

Dr. K. Fisher's Guide to Reptile Defenses

Smaller reptiles make tasty meals for mammals, birds, and larger reptiles. But many of them have clever defenses and could win prizes for their skills in staying alive.

TOP SURVIVOR—frilled lizard

Puffs out its neck frill to look big and scary

SURVIVAL CHAMP—grass snake

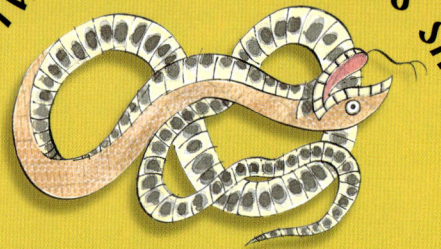

Pretends to be dead so that predators will think it's not fresh enough to eat

WINNING DISGUISE—leaf-tailed gecko

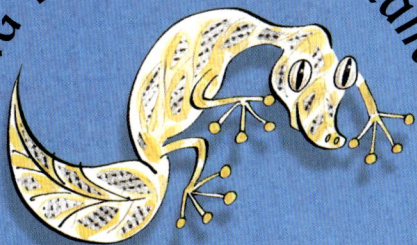

Disguises itself
as a leaf

HIDEAWAY ARTIST—tortoise

Hides inside its own suit
of armor—a strong
protective shell

Dr. K. Fisher's Top Tips

⭐ **DON'T** forget the importance of surprise. Even just sticking out your tongue may scare away a predator.

⭐ **DON'T** complain if you're covered with prickles and spines. These make you almost impossible to eat!

⭐ If you rely on camouflage, **DO** remember to stay still. Your disguise will fail if you move around too much.

9

Here's a troubled rattlesnake

A scary tale

Dear Dr. K. Fisher,
I'm a rattlesnake, and even though I'm one year old, I still play with the rattle at the end of my tail. My friends tell me that rattles are for babies, and they snicker behind my back. But I just can't seem to break the habit. Will I ever grow up?

Snake, Rattle, and Roll,
in the Arizona desert

diamondback
rattlesnake

Dr. K. Fisher
Any problem solved!
1 Diving-in-the-Water
Birdsville 54321

Dear **Snake, Rattle, and Roll,**

It's time to clear up your confusion. Your rattle is not a babyish toy—it's an early-warning system. Your tail is made of dry, scaly ringed segments that buzz loudly when you shake them. When nearby animals hear the noise, they freeze and then move away quietly. They know that you carry a deadly poison that could kill them in a few seconds. Rattling your tail helps you avoid risky fights in which you could get hurt. It also saves your precious poison for another day.

Best regards,

Dr. K. Fisher

gray fox creeping away
from rattlesnake

11

Here's a turtle that needs a rest

I'm so tired!

Dear Dr. K. Fisher,

I'm a female green turtle, and every year I leave my feeding grounds and swim hundreds of miles to lay my eggs on a distant beach. This year, I can't face the long commute, and I'm thinking about laying my eggs on a beach closer to home. The other turtles say that this is a bad idea. What do you think?

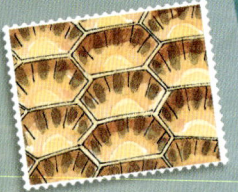

Want an Easy Life,
in the Indian Ocean

green turtle

12

the route to the nesting site

Dr. K. Fisher
Any problem solved!
1 Diving-in-the-Water
Birdsville 54321

Dear **Want an Easy Life,**

I advise you to stick with your old nesting site. Trying to find a new beach is very risky. Will the sand be soft enough to dig a hole? Will your eggs be safe from the tides? How will you manage to find a mate when the males will have already swum to the old site? You're right—it is a long journey. If you're really tired, you could take a year off, as most turtles don't breed every year. But why waste time? Turtles are strong swimmers and your navigation skills are second to none!

Good luck,

Dr. K. Fisher

Made it!

Turn the page for **more about reptile babies . . .**

13

Dr. K. Fisher's Guide to Reptile Babies

Most **baby reptiles** hatch from eggs, but some **develop inside** their mothers' bodies and are born **live**. Only a **few types** of **baby reptiles** are cared for by a **parent**. The **new-baby greeting** cards on **these pages** explain about **four different reptiles**.

Congratulations, mother crocodile!

This proud mother has 30 new crocodile babies. She'll carry them to the water in her strong jaws and protect them for a whole year.

It's a new corn-snake family!

These bouncing boys and girls have just begun to hatch. They are in no hurry to leave the nest and will stay snug inside their eggs for a day or two longer.

Announcing a safe tortoise arrival

The mother laid her eggs in a hole in the ground. Now the baby tortoises are digging their way out, ready to make their way in the world.

New baby sea snakes

These wiggly babies didn't hatch— their mother gave birth to them in the sea. The brave snakelings are ready to swim away on their own.

Dr. K. Fisher's Top Tips

⭐ DO plan for your family: lay eggs in warm soil if you want more boys or in cooler ground for more girls.

⭐ DO lay your eggs on dry land, never in the water.

⭐ DON'T worry about leaving your babies. They have all the skills and instincts they need to survive.

Here's a lizard that wants to soar

Up, up, and away?

Dear Dr. K. Fisher,

I'm a flying lizard, and I live in the rainforest. Every day I thank my lucky stars for my wings, which help me glide through the trees. But I've noticed that birds soar right up to the sky, while I can dive only from tree to tree or down to the ground. How can I fly like a bird?

In a Flap,
in the forest

flying lizard

parrots

Dr. K. Fisher
Any problem solved!
1 Diving-in-the-Water
Birdsville 54321

Dear **In a Flap**,

I am sorry to disappoint you, but you will never be able to fly like a bird. Those "wings" on the sides of your body are just flaps of skin that spread out like a parachute as you jump from tree to tree. Unlike birds, you don't have muscles in your wings and are not strong enough to soar up into the sky. Cheer up, though—try to think of yourself as a fantastic jumper rather than a poor flier and enjoy leaping around the forest.

Yours sincerely,

Dr. K. Fisher

17

cactus plants

Bathroom, please!

Dear Dr. K. Fisher,

I'm a desert tortoise, and something embarrassing has happened to me. I was out in the sun today, and (there's no nice way of saying this) I wet myself. Luckily, I dried off quickly, but I'm sure the other animals must have seen. I almost died of shame! How can I make sure that this never happens again?

Hanging My Head,
in the dunes

18

desert tortoise

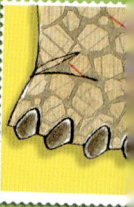

kangaroo rats

Dr. K. Fisher
Any problem solved!
1 Diving-in-the-Water
Birdsville 54321

Dear **Hanging My Head,**

Don't be too hard on yourself. It is so hot in the desert that your body can overheat. In fact, if you stayed out in the sun for too long, you would be baked alive! Wetting yourself is an emergency measure that helps you survive. The liquid cools down your body. This happens very rarely, so forget about it if you can. Usually, you cope well with the heat: by resting in an underground burrow and feeding at the coolest times of the day.

Good luck!

Dr. K. Fisher

cooling off in a **burrow**

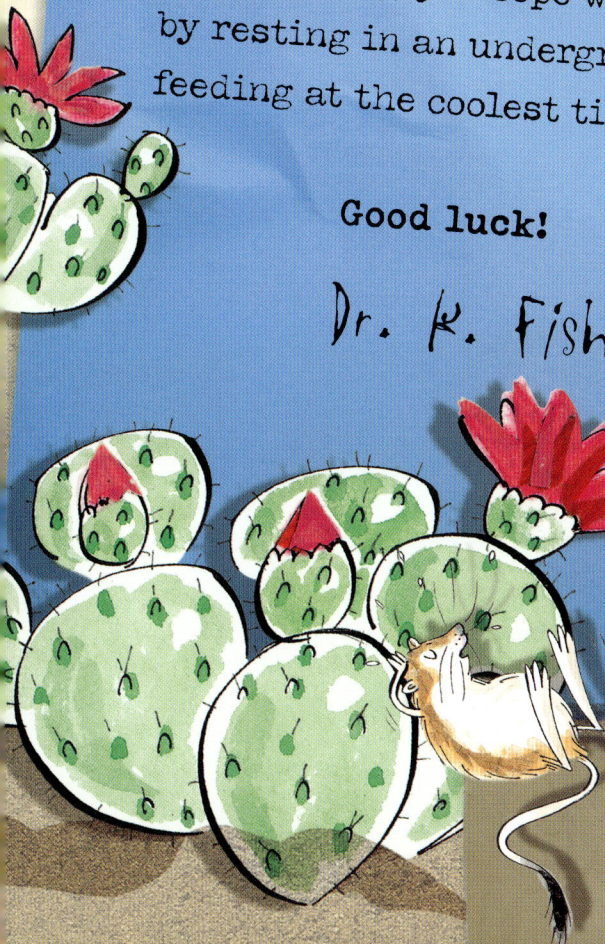

Turn the page for **more** about reptile habitats ...

19

Dr. K. Fisher's Guide to Reptile Habitats

Reptiles **live** all around the world and **have** adapted to many **different** habitats. **The three reptiles here have** special body features that **make them feel** completely at **home** in their chosen habitats.

Web-footed geckos, stand tall in the desert!

We have scaly skin that stops us from drying out and long legs that can lift our bodies high up above the hot sand. We can survive on very little food and water.

Turtles, swim along and "sea" the ocean!

Our smooth shells and strong flippers help us swim fast. We can stay underwater for two hours at a time.

Emerald boas, hang out in the jungle!

Our green skin has bright patches that help us hide in the sunlit leaves. We're so strong that we can climb trees and grip branches all day long.

Dr. K. Fisher's Top Tips

⭐ DO remember that you might face danger if you leave your habitat. A turtle is not very safe on land.

⭐ DON'T worry if other animals share your habitat. You probably eat different foods and make different homes.

⭐ DO try to be flexible to cope with problems. If it's too hot, come out at night. Too cold? Stay under the ground!

21

What a Sight!

Dear Dr. K. Fisher,

I'm a young marine iguana, and I'm worried about my skin. It's very dry and scaly, and there are leathery warts all over my head and prickles down my spine. To top it all off, patches of skin are now beginning to peel off! What on earth is going on?

Feeling Gloomy,
in the Galápagos Islands

THE SHORELINE
OCT. 16TH
MAIL

Dr. K. Fisher

1 Diving-in-the-Water

Birdsville 54321

blue-footed boobies

22

marine iguana

Dr. K. Fisher
Any problem solved!
1 Diving-in-the-Water
Birdsville 54321

Dear **Feeling Gloomy,**

Don't worry—your skin is perfectly normal. All reptiles have tough, dry skin with horny plates, called scales, that stop you from drying out in the sun. Snakes have scales that are very smooth, while tortoises have plates that are fused with bone to make solid shells. Marine iguanas swim in the ocean, so your skin needs to be extra tough in order to protect you from the salt water and hard rocks. As you grow, your old skin peels away, but there's always brighter, glossier skin waiting underneath.

Yours sincerely,

Dr. K. Fisher

crab

brighter
new skin

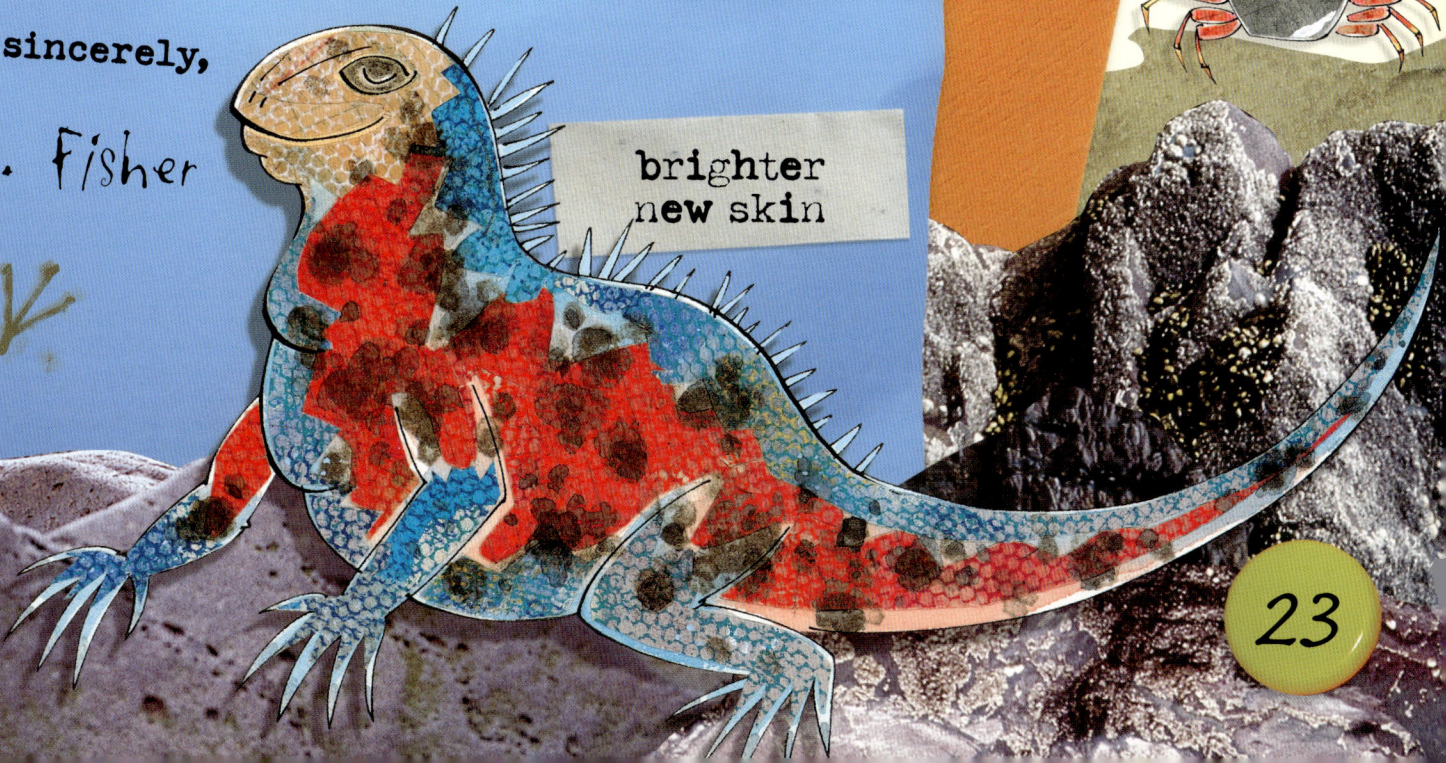

23

Snake in the grass

Dear Dr. K. Fisher,
I'm a rat, and I could use some advice. There's a python that keeps wanting to cuddle me. I'm sure she only wants to be my friend, but the other rats tell me to stay away. I think they're just jealous of our friendship. What do you think?

Feeling Friendly,
in the hills

python

rats

24

URGENT!

Dr. K. Fisher
Any problem solved!
1 Diving-in-the-Water
Birdsville 54321

Dear **Feeling Friendly,**

Stay far away from that python. She is a powerful snake, and rats are one of her favorite foods. Pythons are constrictors, which means that they kill their prey by squeezing it tightly until it cannot breathe. Some other snakes kill by biting with poisonous fangs. All snakes are expert hunters with amazing senses, and they use their forked tongues to pick up the taste of their prey. The other rats are trying to save your life. Please listen to their advice.

Take care,

Dr. K. Fisher

All snakes swallow their prey whole.

Some snakes sniff with forked tongues.

Poisonous snakes bite with fangs.

Turn the page for **more about reptile food . . .**

25

Dr. K. Fisher's Guide to Reptile Food

What's on the menu for reptiles? Most reptiles are carnivores and eat all types of animals. A few are herbivores and prefer to feed on plants.

Meat Eaters

Dinner!

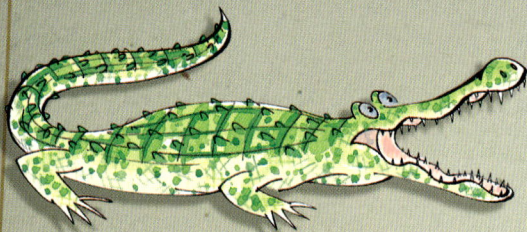

Nile crocodile

antelope

a filling feast from the grasslands

chameleon

grasshoppers

a tasty, high-energy meal

egg-eating snake

eggs

delicious and can be swallowed whole

gavial

fish

a fresh-river delight

Plant Eaters = Lunch!

marine iguana

seaweeds

a sweet and salty snack

tortoise

plants

refreshing, leafy goodness

land iguana

prickly pears

a juicy, thirst-quenching choice

Dr. K. Fisher's Top Tips

 DON'T be in a hurry when you're hunting for food. Successful hunters wait patiently and stay still.

 DON'T expect to catch something every day. A good meal can give you energy for days or even weeks.

 DO try to eat as many types of food as you can. That way, you're more likely to find something to eat.

27

Here's a confused chameleon

me

me again

and again

Still me!

Who am I?

Dear Dr. K. Fisher,
I'm a panther chameleon, and I'm very confused. One minute, I'm green. The next, I'm yellow, or red, or white, or brown. Why does my skin change color like this and which is the real me?

Mixed Up,
in Madagascar

panther chameleon

Dr. K. Fisher
Any problem solved!
Diving-in-the-Water
Birdsville 54321

Dear **Mixed Up,**

Chameleons can transform their skin color for many reasons. If you move into the sunlight, your skin turns pale to reflect the brighter light. If you're cold, your skin gets darker to absorb more heat from the sun. If you're angry, you turn bright red to show that you are ready for a fight. Your skin cells contain grains of color that can be mixed in different combinations as the cells grow or shrink. Usually you're a blotchy green—perfect for hiding in trees.

Good luck!

Dr. K. Fisher

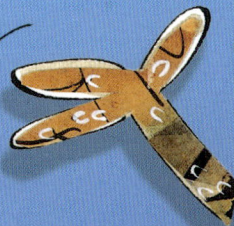

29

Glossary

adapted
Changed in order to cope with the surroundings.

bask
To lie in the sun in order to warm up.

breed
To produce babies.

camouflage
A shape, color, or pattern that helps an animal hide.

carnivore
An animal that eats other animals.

cartilage
A rubbery substance in the body; also called gristle. Bones and cartilage are found in reptile skeletons.

cell
A tiny part of an animal's body.

cold-blooded
Having blood that warms up or cools down depending on the outside temperature. Reptiles are cold-blooded.

constrictor
A type of snake that kills its prey by squeezing it.

digest
To break down food so that the body can use it.

disguise
A shape, color, or pattern that makes an animal look like something else to help it escape from danger.

fang
A special type of sharp, pointed tooth.

flipper
A leg that is perfectly shaped for swimming.

habitat
The place where an animal lives.

herbivore
An animal that eats plants.

instinct
An animal's natural knowledge of the things it needs to do in order to survive.

liquid
Something that is wet and flows easily, like water.

mate
To join with a partner to breed (have babies).

moisture
A small amount of water.

navigation
Finding the way to a specific place.

parachute
An object, a little like an umbrella, that helps someone jump from a big height and fall slowly and safely.

predator
An animal that hunts and kills other animals (prey) for food.

prey
An animal that is eaten by other animals (predators).

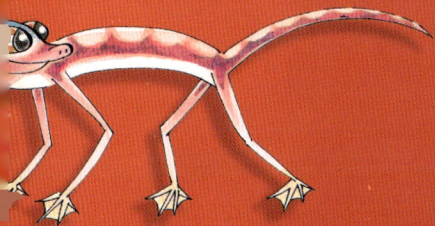

rainforest
A thick, tropical forest. Another word for *rainforest* is *jungle*.

reptile
A cold-blooded animal with tough, scaly skin.

scale
One of the thin protective plates that cover a reptile's skin and make it strong and tough.

snakeling
A baby snake.

temperature
How hot or cold something is.

transforming
Changing.

tropics
Parts of the world near the equator where the weather is always hot.

Index